POTHOLES
IN
MEMORY LANE

Richard Allen Anderson

Vabella Publishing
P.O. Box 1052
Carrollton, Georgia 30112
www.vabella.com

©Copyright 2016 Richard Anderson

All rights reserved. No part of the book may be reproduced or utilized in any form or by any means without permission in writing from the author. All requests should be addressed to the publisher.

Manufactured in the United States of America

13-digit ISBN 978-1-942766-25-4

Library of Congress Control Number 2016915778

10 9 8 7 6 5 4 3 2 1

DEDICATION

to us

Richard's Other Books

Another Season Spent
(poetry) Vabella Publishing, 2013

The Adventures of Diggerydoo and Taller Too
(for children) Vabella Publishing, 2016

CONTENTS

Forewarning   1
Potholes in Memory Lane   5

    ONE
Country Roads   9
distant memories   10
yesterday's dreams   10
faded photograph   10
Echoes   11
first light   14
bright flashes   14
early morning fog   15
August evening   15
faded leaves   15
A Tenuous Tenacity   16
Openings   19
On the Subject of Waiting   20

CONTENTS (cont)

TWO

Mr. Law Abiding	25
Spinster	27
Sea Dog	27
Cold Cash	28
Memory Problems?	28
Not Too Bright Bob	29
Death of a Member	30
Looking Back	30
International Relations	31
Short Marriage	31
Blondes Have More Fun	32
Female Viagra	32
Campus Life	33
The Modern Way	33
Ill-suited	34
God Made Me Do It	34

THREE

Birthday Celebration	37
Melody of Love	38
Alone	39
Falling	40
Pas de Deux	42
Senior Center Moment	44
Transition	46
Bright and Tarnished	47
Pledge for Today	48

CONTENTS (cont)

FOUR

Years Truly	51
Shadows at Dawn	55
Words	59
About Poetry	60
Tokens	61
Beneath	64
Parodo (parody on Basho)	65
Closing the Book	66
Emoticon World	66
Not A-Mused	66
Quid Pro Quo	67
Unfulfilled	68

FIVE

Attention Getters	71
Death by Drunk	72
Torment	72
Remembering Nizear	73
Rules of the Game	76
The Late	76
Emotaku	77
On the Subject of Death	78
Obituary	79

CONTENTS (cont)

SIX

Something to Chew On	83
Dishes: 1 and 2	84
Expectations: 1, 2, 3	85
Easter Morning	86
Easter Afternoon	87
Choir Practice	88
Moonstruck	89
A Stroll on the Beach	90
Nocturnes	91
stone sober	92
fleeting shadow	92

SEVEN

Vector/Scalar	95
Space and Time	96
Summer Harvest	97
Introspection	99
Holding On	100
Twenty-eight Days	101
81	105
Old Poet's Lament	106
Eighty-Three	108
Eleven Fifty-nine	110
Train Wreck	112
Watch Out	113

CONTENTS (cont)

EIGHT

Ravens	117
Crows	118
Journey's End	119
brown lawns	121
slow awakening	121
tulips	121
fat crows	122
two cardinals	122
Gourmet Dog	123
Dinosaur Divorce	123
Moonlight Serenade	124
After the Storm	125
Fish Tale	126
Frieda Croaks	128

CONTENTS (cont)

ADDENDUMB

Your Pick	131
Boris the Talking Horse	132
Medical Alert	133
Scope This Out	
Diagnosis	
Aftershock	
If	134
Stormy	135
Suppose	136
Stretching	137
Carter's Pills	138

AFTERTHOUGHTS — 139

ACKNOWLEDGEMENTS — 141

PARTING SHOT — 143

REFERENCES — 145

Forewarning

There are two kinds of people: those who read forwards and those who do not. They are (forwards, that is) non-essential, after all. I, for one, have often skipped these prosaic condiments in my hurry to get to the main course. But often I return to the Forward after sampling the fare. There I find clues as to what may lie behind the content of the pages I have just read and what might have been in the mind of the author when she or he wrote them.

So here is a little direct talk between me, the writer, and you, the reader.

Feel free to respond to wordwaggler@gmail.com.

Much of the poetry you will read on these pages is intensely personal, whether in reaction to some large or small wonder of nature or to an event or circumstance that has profoundly affected my life or that of a loved one.

In general, my poetry is down to earth, a celebration of life, an attempt to describe some small facet of life on the indescribably beautiful and diverse planet we share with 7.5 billion others, as we twist and float in a vast and incomprehensible, universe.

Some of the verses have been prompted by more or less severe adversities, notably the precipitous decline in my spouse's physical and mental health in recent years or the recognition of one's own failing abilities that accompany the blessing of advancing years.

>   my poetry sings
>   the anthems of
>   an eighty year old man

It is only natural, then, that my perspective is more retrospective than visionary, at times cynical, at other times optimistic. My intent is simple: to share these personal experiences and emotions that others, young and old and in between, may have in common.

I am a smorgasbord guy. When it comes to dining or reading or writing, I like to mix it up. I have a need to experiment, to explore, to try something new. That said, I still relish the old standbys. I take comfort in the roast beef with carrots and oven-browned potatoes, the meatloaf, the chicken noodle soup, the biscuits and gravy, though even here I may introduce some new ingredient, some new twist.

My writing, like my cooking, is not based on secret recipes or formulas. This does pose some risk, of course. Not every attempt is palatable. Moreover, what is new to me may be tried and true to someone else. I take pleasure in researching ancient and exotic writings, learning how they exert their special magic, then tweaking, bending and, at times, abusing the sanctified rules of form or content.

Certain poetic forms are more intentionally personal than others. Among these are several forms adapted by the West from ancient Asian poetry. Haiku, comprising only 17 syllables or fewer is an example that has been described by poet laureate, Billy Collins, as "powerful little assertions of the poet's very existence." Haibun, describes a deeply personal experience by combining prose and verse.

Few poetic forms are more appropriate than the five-line Limerick in presenting human foibles and frailties.

You will find a smattering of these brief, humorous verses on these pages. You will also find tanka, another five-line poem of only 31 syllables adapted to both humor and serious intent.

I draw inspiration from poets as diverse as Walt Whitman, Robert Frost and Shel Silverstein, to name only a few, and amuse myself using forms ranging from free verse to older, formal structures.

You will find on these pages both prose and poetry and composites of the two. You will find some classic forms. You will find other writings with no precedent in style to my knowledge. I take to heart the words of Richard Gilbert in writing about haiku that "innovation is the lifeblood of this art form . . . ," and I apply the concept to all of my poetry and prose.

You will find shorter poems and longer poems—quick snacks or something more substantial to chew on. Pick and choose. Fill your plate, but savor each morsel before moving down the buffet line. I hope you are tempted to taste them all and that you find some to your liking. Feel free to return often for seconds.

The theme of life as a journey, a moving changeable feast is a common thread woven throughout this collection of poems. We will travel along some city streets, some winding country roads and perhaps a dark alley or two. I hope you enjoy your journey along a few of life's pathways with me, but be careful of the potholes.

Richard Allen Anderson
September, 2016

Potholes in Memory Lane

Near the end of our journey
As we sit in a rocker
Looking backward
Not forward
At the paths we have chosen
Hilly, winding and twisted
Over tortuous detours
All the joys of the voyage
Arise in our memories
With our hopeful minds
Filling
The potholes in memory lane

ONE

Country Roads

Open fields on the outskirts of our small town near the western Georgia border have lain fallow and unworked for generations. The land seems to sing with subdued voices of the past—black workers humming and chanting while bent over dry, prickly cotton bolls on a hot late-August afternoon, echoes of the gee and haw of a farmer guiding his mules and plow, the cough and chug of a one-cylinder John Deere.

Weathered gray barns and sheds, dilapidated reminders of distant days, teeter precariously alongside the rural byways. Late on dusky autumn evenings, small rafters of wild turkey emerge into the long shadows of the surrounding woodlands to scavenge barren fields. Ravens gather to conspire in the dimming light of day. And slowly, silently nature reaches out to reclaim her rightful providence.

black birds bob and strut
on rusted tin roofs, below
only goldenrod

jet trails high above
intersecting and fading
distant memories

shells on the beach
fragments shattered and worn
yesterday's dreams

faded photograph
bright memories
dimly perceived

Echoes

A house, once a home, still stands
on Google Maps, satellite view,
flanked by faithful aging neighbors.
The alley that I walked to school, K thru 6,
now dead-ends into a vacant lot,
a stand of verdant, full grown trees.
A century-old host to generations
of unrelated families, the house still stands.

No garden fills the yard where Dad
grew summer vegetables for his family of six—
a few dollars saved from his meager pay
to be used to buy the children's shoes
or tires for the family sedan, the '32 black Buick
used only for an occasional Sunday outing
or that one week of summer vacation
not too far from home.

No smoke meanders from the second-story windows
open to the chill Wisconsin winter air as when Mom
fried up platters of delicious potato pancakes—
served always with fresh applesauce.
But save room for dessert, fresh baked devils food cake
still warm from the oven, topped with creamy frosting
washed down with a large glass of cold milk.
No meal at this house was complete without dessert.

Echoes (cont.)

Listen carefully and you may hear
voices of the past that echo in its rooms
voices more familiar to me than my own
some silent now for thirty years or more.
Children's voices—squabbling, arguing,
whispering secrets, or laughing at play.
The quiet voices of my parents in their bed
discussing whatever parents discuss.

What is bothering you? You haven't said a word.
I got a promotion. And a raise to $95 a month . . . .
We'll have to save up to get you a new suit.
I might be retired by then. Maybe for my burial.
Can we drive out to the farm on Sunday?
I'm not sure we have enough ration stamps for gas.
The war. Is it ever going to end? . . .
Like the late night fog, silence settles in.

Voices of friends or family just stopping by
to say hello or maybe stay for pot luck dinner.
And voices of unseen friends borne on waves—
Saturday afternoon at the Met, an evening
with Fred Allen, an invitation to the inner sanctum,
a fireside chat with FDR, reassuring, encouraging—
we sit enthralled, cross legged on the living room floor
facing the console radio, listening to voices.

Echoes (cont.)

A century-old house still stands
on a quiet street—home
to another generation of modern sounds
and voices, singing out their humanity,
adding their vibrations to those earlier
embedded in the bones of the old dwelling.
Voices emanate and echo from the walls.
Listen. I can hear them clearly now.

first light of day
reaches the shore
on gentle rolling waves

bright flashes
under the lily pads
goldfish being koi

early morning fog
lies in wait for the dawn
not one green leaf stirs

August evening
warm breezes turning cool
first breath of Autumn

faded leaves dancing
on icy, barren branches
Happy New Year!

A Tenuous Tenacity

To say I am a non-believer would be somewhat incorrect.
I have pored and I have pondered,
considered and contemplated
many of the World's religions and philosophies,
and though I've racked and searched my head,
I hang my hat on none of them.

I have been baptized and confirmed
in one of the Christian faiths.
A priest of still another pronounced me
united until death with my mate
(as if I needed his pronouncement as assurance).
I have spent countless, restless hours listening

to the Gospel, Parables and Praise of the Almighty,
the one and only true God.
I have frequently found friends
amongst those congregations,
gentle folks in general, who care
more for the welfare of my soul than I.

I quietly accept the good intentions of their blessings
while I critically question the very basis of their beliefs.
I have searched for meaning in the dogma, ritual and
fantasies of their faith
but cannot accept what they so ardently embrace
and hold to be the only truth, the light, salvation, the way.

Tenacity (cont)

I have wandered the dark alleys of existentialism too.
One cannot find comfort in the arms of an uncaring
universe, and in the end,
comfort may be more compelling than the truth.
But to say I am an unbeliever would be
somewhat incorrect.

In the face of corruption and greed,
of brutal inhumanities,
beheadings, rape, torture, murder and maiming of children
and defenseless animals in the name of the one true god,
I somehow maintain my belief in
the goodness of humankind.

Can I deny that we are more than mud and DNA,
that some force, a human and humane spirit
and intelligence exists
betwixt the foibles, frailties and derelictions
of the species Homo sapiens,
a force for good, perhaps akin to love?

Or is there a gene for courage, kindness and compassion,
an ancient permutation to the evolving double helix,
an errant protein fragment that some of us do not possess?
Can mere biochemistry explain the entirety of who we are?

Tenacity (cont)

Perhaps it is the children with their innocence intact
who have not yet learned to hate and to despise the others
those alter humans who are not us and we not they—
the children who feed and fuel my unfounded faith.

I weep for their vulnerability, their ultimate perversion.
I am inadequate to defend their inchoate spirits, to bring
the Truth, or even comfort, neatly boxed and ribboned
to be opened at their end-of-adolescence party.

They will find their way down life's shadowed pathways
seeking somehow to bring meaning to their existence.
Some may find satisfaction in simple service to another
amidst the inhumanity. Should they search for more?

And what god shall I curse, watching my beloved wither,
frailties increasing, encroaching into limbs and mind
that once were beautiful, vigorous and strong as she,
while her tenacious and childlike spirit will not succumb.

To say I am a non-believer would be,
in some ways, incorrect.

Openings

Our Lady of Perpetual Help, OLPH to all except Father Raphe, is a small outpost of the Catholic Church on the rural periphery of Carrollton, Georgia. Cattle graze in fenced pastures across the quiet country road from the humble church. The foundation of the church rests on land that also once was farmed.
Land for the church, the rectory and a small cemetery were a gift from seemingly unlikely patrons, actress Susan Hayward and her husband, Floyd Chalkley, a Carrollton business man and rancher.
Susan and Floyd lie at rest in a small memorial cove just a few steps from the narthex of OLPH church and slightly apart from the greater church yard that is the final resting place of many departed faithful parishioners. Today, on a gray, misty winter morning, two bright canopies shelter freshly dug trenches and complement the colorful polyester bouquets that perpetually decorate the gravesites.
During the mass, the good Father recites two new names on the list for special intention prayers.

new openings
in the quaint necropolis
welcoming old souls

On the Subject of Waiting

waiting
like gravity
bends time

impatient souls
await the coming
of the visiting priest

Waiting (cont)

consider
the day a success
whenever you have a BM

the geezers have finally arrived
and what a great surprise—
the geezers is us

TWO

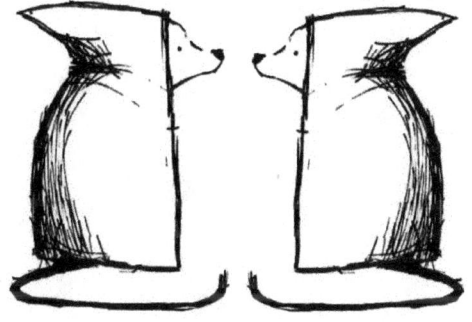

Mr. Law Abiding

Every now and then
I get the urge to sin
Behaving well can be so boring
Angels hover, never soaring

No monstrous act
No devilish pact
With motives mystifying
And headlines horrifying

Just something minor—
A misdemeanor—
Would be quite satisfying
For Mr. Law Abiding

Mr. Law Abiding (cont)

But, if I wander on a whim
Would redemption's chance be really slim?
Should I purloin a lowly melon
Would I become a lifelong felon?

When my darker moments vent
Should I tremble and repent?
Why does the very thought of badness
Not fill by soul with somber sadness?

So, I still seek some evil-doing
Perhaps enough to bring
A quick adrenaline high
But no matter how I try

I'm stuck with Mr. Law Abiding

Spinster

There was a very old spinster
Who thought marriage and sex were quite sinister
But she married at last
To a love from her past
And the honeymoon just about finished her

Sea Dog

There was an old sea dog named Rex
Who thought often and long about sex
But his journeys at sea
Gave him no company
Of the opposite sex—poor Rex

Cold Cash

There was an ambitious young feller
Who aspired to become a bank teller
But wealth went to his head
And he robbed one instead
And stashed all the cash in the cellar

Memory Problems?

Agha Khan from Istanbul Turkey
Found his memory was spotty and quirky
He popped on his fez
And fergat where it wez
'til it drove him completely berzerky

Not Too Bright Bob

Bob Jones drove with less than half his brain
To think and drive was really too much strain
Now Jones' bones lie beneath this sad but true refrain
"Too dumb to turn his lights on in the rain."

Death of a Member

I was sad when poor Willy died
He took many long years to subside
Now his nerves are all shot
No sensation he's got
He no longer is this pilgrim's pride

Looking Back

He knew 'twas no longer an omen
He now was the slowest of slow men
Though he used to run fast
Now he always was last
But he could still write a silly old poem

International Relations

An alluring juene fille in Paree
Felt lively jumps in her tummy
She thought back to the night
When it all seemed so right
With that salesman from East Germany

Short Marriage

A lady barkeep from Poughkeepsie
One day married a wandering gypsy
She was completely bereft
When the next day he left
The tipsy gypsy'd drunk all her good whiskey

Blondes Have More Fun

He married a lovely brunette
Owned a house and a car and a pet
But she scolded and nagged
'til his clothes he all bagged
And ran off with a blonde named Evette

Female Viagra

There was a young woman named Sue
With sex wanted nothing to do
But she tried the new pill
And now thinks that she will
Libido in both pink and blue

Campus Life

There was an old Baptist sorority
Well known for its rigid sobriety
But they flirted with boys
And knew all the joys
Of a night of back-seat frivolity

The Modern Way

Friends with benefits is the modern thing
Casual living with an occasional fling
No commitment for all your days
Easy to go your separate ways
Like matrimony without the ring

Ill-suited

Mrs. Clause said she'd give him the boot
If he didn't look good on his route
He checked Amazon first
And e-Bay, which was worse
No 14X red fur-lined suits

God Made Me Do It

A guy named Noah once built an ark
His wife Noamah thought it a lark
So Noah, he told her
With a dove on each shoulder
Soon there won't be no place to park

THREE

Birthday Celebration

My love is eighty-five today.
I'll get her some flowers
And sit by her side
And sing Happy Birthday
As one candle glows
On a chocolate cupcake.
I'll ask if her boyfriends
Out-number her toes
Just to be funny, though
Everyone knows she had many a beau
When she told me she loved me
All those eons ago.
Then I'll kiss her sweet lips
And her cheeks and her eyes
And tell her I love her
But it's such a surprise that
My love is eight-five today.

Melody of Love

One two three, one two three. Open, open, close.
Dolly loves to dance. When we started to date in college, she did her best to instruct me in the musical maneuvers of the two-step, the tango, the polka, the samba, the foxtrot, the waltz.
We had our own song, The Melody of Love, that I faithfully requested at every school dance. Dance became integral with "us." We danced at our wedding. We danced at our children's weddings.

Twenty years ago, a brain tumor claimed the hearing in her left ear. Gradually, the music faded also from her right. Now she no longer hears the melody, no longer feels the beat. The relentless, uncaring march of time has stolen her grace and balance.
Now we dance holding tight, feet stationary, bodies swaying to the rhythm of our hearts, remembering.

as if to ask
is this our song
her quiet smile

Alone

She doesn't like to be alone
Needs reassurance
That I am near
Complains
Calls out, Where are you?
Where on earth have you been?
Though I am just around the corner
In another room of our small home

So, I sit with her in the afternoon
Or lie beside her in the early morning hours
Thinking
I need to do this
Or that

Falling

The first time she fell we blamed the medications. Narcotic plunderers of mindfulness and pain. Her blank eyes, unaware of the damage she had done, the broken teeth, the bloodied face. Numb to the pain.

Time heals. The mind forgets, avoids. The next fall, months later, is less severe. The carpet cushions her landing. She berates her clumsiness. No drugs to blame now.

Infrequent falls, small aftershocks, send tremulous warnings. Again, and then again. No brittle bones broken until she cracks the orbit of her eye, another tooth is shattered.

"You need to use the walker at all times." And she does. Then three falls in two days. I struggle to help her off the floor.
"We can't keep meeting like this."
We laugh, and our eyes fill with questions.
"I will get a wheelchair for you now."

"What's wrong with me?" she asks.
The words are halting and unsure, like her Tim Conway shuffle.

Falling (cont)

"No new stroke," the neurologist intones with certainty and satisfaction, "but she has lost all sensation and motor control of her lower legs. I can't suggest a treatment."

She attempts bravely to perform the exercises that may maintain some function in her withering muscles, allow some greater scope to the shrinking spectrum of her daily activities.

The La-Z-Boy is her sanctuary. The television is her ersatz companion. She does not like to be alone, calls my name when I leave the room until, reluctantly, I return.

oh, there you are
come sit here with me
numb to the pain

Pas de Deux
(a dance duet)

She loves to dance.
Considered it for a vocation once.
Or might have been a fly-girl,
but her mother wouldn't sign.

Attended Teacher's College instead. More practical.
We met there and dated. She taught me
how to dance. The waltz, the polka, the two-step,
others without names.

She had many other beaus, but she waited
while I wasn't ready, while I served my military duty.
I finally proposed on one knee with the solitary diamond
I had purchased in Amsterdam. She said yes.

We danced at our wedding reception
before our weekend honeymoon in the Windy City.
She counted and I moved my feet.
One two three. One two three.

Now we have a ritual dance.
She does not move her feet as I hold her close and lift
from the wheelchair into the Lazyboy
and raise her lifeless legs.

Pas de Deux (cont)

She settles back.
I punch the remote to find *Dancing With the Stars*.
She smiles, and I wonder, in her silent world,
does she remember?

Does she still count for me,
one two three,
one two three,
as we dance our quiet Pas de Deux?

Senior Center Moment

The sound of numbered marbles
Rattling in a wired cage
Stills the talk around the tables
Hushes voices hoarse with age.

We all hear the caller's voice to say
O'er the dwindling murmur of the crowd
Are you ready? Are you here to play?
Yes! But, call 'em slowly, call 'em loud.

Then here we go, and your first number is
The little baby, little old B-one.
Can you hear me call the numbers,
And is everybody having fun?

The next number is the old gray man
O-seventy five, O-seven-five,
And we've covered the entire span
From babe in arms to glad to be alive.

My darling wife loves to play this game
Of chance, perhaps to win a prize.
Though she's deaf she loves it all the same.
As each number's picked, she strains her eyes

To read the caller's moving lips:
It's the little train, he says, I-twenty-two,
And all the players echo back the quip:
Two-two, too-too, toot toot.

Senior Center Moment (cont)

My poor dear wife is not amused
By this ritual of fantasy.
Extraneous voices leave her confused
By humor she cannot hear nor see.

The next one flies like a silent bird
Past straining eyes and deafened ears
To stay unseen, to remain unheard
And I nudge and point to allay her fears.

N-forty-four, N four-four
She glances at me for confirmation
Then fills that space, needs just one more
And she's wired with anticipation.

G-sixty- three. G-six-three.
She glances again, I shake my head;
She frowns and sighs dejectedly.
The caller selects a numbered bead

Turns the orb and brings it to his eye . . .
I-thirty, he calls, I-three-O!
Eyes on fire, her hand shoots high—
Bingo. . . Bingo. . . Bingo!

Transition

my wife
my lover
my enigma
my nemesis
my best friend
my support
my partner
and then
my child
my life

Bright and Tarnished

your bright mind
your childlike soul
your world of silence

one hundred spoons
neatly hung behind glass doors
tarnished memories

Pledge for Today

Today
After all the years, the tears
The fears, the foibles
The love, the joy
we've shared,

Today
Will be our very best.

My fear, frustration,
Quiet desperation
May sometimes
Masquerade as Anger
But not today.

Today, I will sincerely strive to be
The sweetest motherfucker on this earth.

FOUR

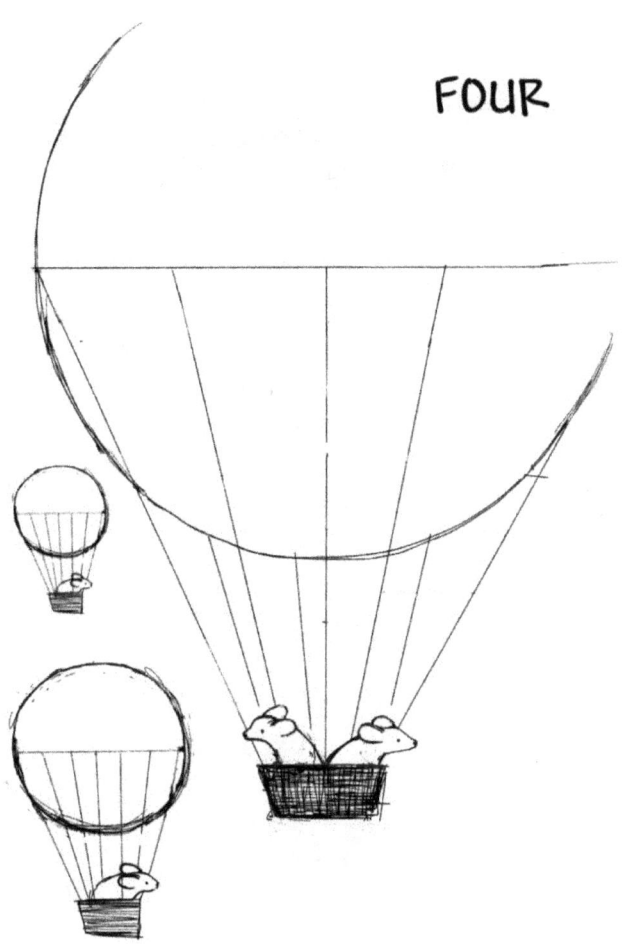

Years Truly

When did humans first attempt to capture time, to count the passing days and seasons, to dare to think of a future that might mimic or be coda to what had gone before?

When did they first observe and somehow note the regular patterns of the powerful Sun in a clear or clouded sky or the phases of the feeble Moon? When did they first find courage to confront the fearsome universe of stars and wandering planets to predict their movements in the blackened sky?

Without numbers, how did they count the fleeting days of their existence, the accumulated sunrises and sunsets as the planet earth twisted on its axis and hurtled through the dark vacuum of space, circuiting the life-giving star that we now call the Sun? When did they first comprehend their journey?

Millennia followed upon millennia while the race evolved, still servant to and never master of time. Yet, today we capture time in small square boxes, neatly named and numbered. We page forward in time to plan the future or turn back to recall the past. We do not question why the days of the week number seven, not five nor eleven, or why we even have a timespan called a week. Why is the span of time we call a month no more than 31 days in length but as few as 28; why does February get short shrift but special treatment every few years.

Years Truly (cont)

Our imperfect calendar retains many cosmic qualities from the ancient past. Is the seven day week in honor of the seven heavenly bodies whose names they carry or is it ordained by God's commandment as some would assert?

Even though the span of time we call a month approximates the duration of a lunar cycle, we do not watch with awe, as the ancients did, while the moon develops horns or waxes back night by night to shine bright and full upon us with reflected light. We merely turn a page.

We measure the passing of our days and weeks, months and years with often mundane, if still intensely human, activity. We mark our calendars with celebrations, observations, remembrances. We look forward to repeating the past.

January
taking down the tree
resolutions, brand new calendar

February
under leaden skies
gray, barren branches

March
icy winds
hopeful humble daffodils

Years Truly (cont)

        April
azaleas, dogwoods, tulips,
forgotten resolutions. Taxes

        May
bluebirds, fresh flowers
wilt on fresh gravesites

        June
soft scents, warm breezes, I dos,
new tie for Dad

        July
the Flag marches by
rat a tat tat

        August
a drop of my sweat
falls on my young grandson

        September
tiny yellow jackets, eager
to drown in hummingbird nectar

        October
autumn gold and red
mottled, shriveled, dead

Years Truly (cont)

November
all thankful
but the turkey

December
warm fire, quiet snowfall,
she smiles wrapping my gift

Shadows at Dawn

Homo X, with dreadful reverence,
draws up his muscled arms
points ahead toward the east
extending long and bristled fingers
toward the magical aurora
and as the golden rim appears
raises voice to sustain a sound
o o o o o o o o o
a simple sound
suffuse with complex, primitive emotion:
awe and gratitude, fear and pleasure.

The small band of huddled beings
emerging from the cavern's mouth
sends forth a joyful, manic chorus
across the grassy plain
into the distant shadowed forest—
O O O O O O O O O . . .

They stand erect and elevate their arms
join their fingers above their dimly lighted faces.
Another day to hunt and forage.
Another day to risk at living.

Homo X leaps upon a high flat rock
his place of honor, his platform to survey
and lead the morning mystic ritual.
The first bright rays surmount the trees, illuminate
his fearsome face, his massive chest, his extended limbs.

Shadows at Dawn (cont)

An unforetold, unwanted force stirs within his brain,
an awareness of a furtive presence deep within.
His ferocious eyes dart and race,
absorb the full extent of his own being.
His strong hands press against the turmoil in his skull.
A sound stirs unsummoned within his throat—
Aaah Aaah

The sound persists within him, seeking to escape
forcing his heavy lips apart
then bursts forth to startle and bewilder
the others and himself. Ah!
And then another even stranger sound. Ya!

A simian smile distorts his face.
With lips parted and drawn back
ahya he whispers, ahya, then shouts
Ahya. Ahya. Ahya!

He whirls about to face the fearful group.
Sunlight exaggerates the shadow of his broad shoulders
and makes serpents of his upraised arms upon the ground.

He points a finger at his chest
and now forcefully, willfully, articulates
the sylables of self-image—Ahya!
With wonder in his newfound power—Ahya. Ahya.
Concept burgeons into Comprehension.

Shadows at Dawn (cont)

He jumps with simple joy, high in the still air,
returns to his haunches, springs high again, again.
He beholds the sunlit, shadowed brows
of his gathered species-homo family.

They stare agape in fearful apprehension.

Homo X descends
from his altar of enlightenment
pervaded now with understanding
a new connection fused, a virgin neuron pathway
somewhere within his primal brain.

He grasps the hand of each fellow being
to place it against its own naked breast and,
eyes ablaze, speaks the magic syllables—

Ahya.

First one,
then two or three,
not comprehending
but submissively compliant
attempt the sound
Aah. Aah. Ahya. Ahya.

The embryonic thought ascends
displacing shadows of ignorance.
They slap their arms, their chests,
their now wide-eyed faces
acknowledging with ape-like grins
their dawning understanding
their linking of thought and sound.

Shadows at Dawn (cont)

A word is born
one simple utterance:

Within it
the seeds of human perception
communication, language, intelligence.

Within it
the plays and poetry
of Sophocles, Shakespeare, Ibsen.

Within it
the analects of Confucius
the Magna Carta,
the Declaration of Independence
the Communist Manifesto.

Within it
an infinity of unimagined worlds.

Words

Holy-Moley, carbon copy, many *words* from the past
I can't remember when I've heard most of them last.

Are these expressions all now passé,
No more to be seen by the light of today?

I know them all well; quote most of them still,
Small wonder the grandkids think my mind's a bit ill.

Their own bright jargon, the phrases they speak,
Sound as foreign to me as Urdu or Greek.

But some things remain that we all comprehend
Told by our actions, need no words in the end.

These are the constants: truth, honor and love—
Passed up family tree branches to generations above.

So, let the words fall like the leaves in autumn
If the kids just remember the best that we taught 'em.

About Poetry

images arise
from words printed on a page
poetic wizardry

why haiku?
tiny moments
fill a lifetime

my poetry sings
the anthems of an
eighty year old man

Tokens

The brave but hapless pawn
with limited ability, moves haltingly,
feet firmly planted, one step at a time,
dreaming not to leap nor soar,
seeing only the fearful face that looms
just before his watchful eyes.
He is the first to go,
sacrificed with little note
little regret
to the progress of the game.

The recalcitrant rook,
reluctant to leave his corner
of the world, has potential to go far
is thwarted, blocked and stymied,
resisting new moves he vacillates—
back and forth, side to side,
a holding pattern
without purpose
without progress.

Tokens (cont)

How intriguing that
the cunning bishop
in his pointed mitre
moves only obliquely,
devious and diagonal
to the flow of the game.
Few question his power,
a rival to the throne.

The trusted knight is granted
special powers by virtue
only of the agile steed he mounts.
Resplendent in his armor
leaping high above the fray
cutting quickly
left or right
before retreating.

How boundlessly dissimilar
The Royal Couple
from their regal mates.

Tokens (cont)

The vapid, clueless King
shuffles here and there
never distant from his throne,
no notion
where next to turn,
wary and fearful
as a nervous mouse
unable to defend
his kingdom or himself.

But Oh!
The Glorious Queen—
watch out for her.
She has all the moves.
She protects her monarch mate
as she would a poor defenseless child:
With all her wily wit
With all her hopeful heart
With all her steadfast soul

until at last

Checkmate.

Beneath

There was an aspiring young poet
Who found limericks stuck in his throat
He wrote eloquently
With great dignity
But lim'ricks were way far below it

Parodo
(parody on Basho)

Matsuo Basho lived in 17th century Japan, composing poetry and teaching while wandering extensively across the countryside on foot.
He is the mostly widely recognized master of the haiku form and also innovated haibun in which he linked descriptive prose with haiku.
Basho's poetic style transformed haiku poetry in describing nature in the briefest, simplest and most striking terms without adhering to existing formal conventions. Some of his work also displays a quiet sense of humor
His creativity, reverence for nature and irreverence for established convention and the foibles of humans make him a hero to me.
I salute him with this irreverent haiku-like verse.

Basho once opined
I am not averse to verse
just so it is terse

Closing the Book

reluctant farewell
protagonists and villains
slowly laid to rest,
disappearing, once again
between covers of the book

In This Emoticon World

on my Facebook page
Likes are good, Comments better
and now Reactions—
emotions with just a stroke
Words may soon be obsolete

Not A-mused

the reluctant words
need cajoling to emerge
but my stubborn muse
won't pick up my urgent calls
I hate the obstinate bitch

Quid Pro Quo

A tiny bug crawled across the page
And I squashed it with my thumb.
Do I deserve Mother Nature's rage?
Was my reaction dumb?
Bug body now is just a smudge.
Mother Nature, do you hold a grudge?

Suppose, just suppose, on some other day
I happened to land in another's way.
Might I then get the fickle finger of fate
And be on my way to the heavenly gate
Just as quickly and with as little thought
As when I squashed the bug that sought
Its lonely way across my page?

Unfulfilled

There was an old poet named Dick
Who tried to write a limerick
He ran out of time
To find a good rhyme
So he left it for you to finish

FIVE

Attention Getters

radiologist:
. . . a spot on your X-ray . . .
we should biopsy

her voice
studiously calm
your son . . . accident

Death by Drunk

a bright spring morning
blissful, waiting for the bus
thinking about lunch
the impact struck him lifeless
the drunk driver unaware

Torment

his broken young face
at rest on the pale pillow
still etched now in death
by his brief torment and fear
his father gasps in despair

Remembering Nizzear

We learned about the murder when my iPhone chirped with a text from my daughter.

Did you hear about the shooting?
He was in Andy's class.
What if the shooter comes to school?
Lock your doors!

Little more was known then but that a boy was dead—shot once in the head, and that the boy, who had celebrated his 13th birthday the day before, lived in the apartment complex adjacent to our small subdivision. News reports described him as an excellent student and athlete, cheerful, well-behaved and well-liked—always smiling. His name was Nizzear, and though he lived less than half a mile distant, we lived a world apart.

The apartment complex where Nizzear lived is a failed student housing project turned low-income housing occupied by black and Hispanic families in a community where these "minorities" make up more than half the population. The police report that the complex has been increasingly troubled with criminal and gang activity. It stands in stark contrast to our long-established subdivision of small, neat homes that is, for the most part, a defacto retirement community of senior adults. The only children we see are those visiting their grandparents. Neighbors know neighbors. Neighbors help neighbors. It is a quiet place where doors are often left unlocked.

Remembering Nizzear (cont)

No one witnessed the shooting, with the possible exception of the victim. No one called the police. On a tip, the police arrested a 17-year-old black boy the next day. Some days later two young adults, one male and one female, were arrested and also charged with the murder. The adult male and the teenager allegedly entered the unlocked apartment at an early morning hour and shot Nizzear as he lay in bed.

No clear motive has been established. Robbery was apparently not a motive. Speculation points to mistaken identity. A teen-age boy living nearby, perhaps a rival gang member, may have been the intended victim. One wonders how soundly he sleeps now.

While the three alleged perpetrators remain in jail with no bail, the police continue to probe for a motive. The murder is incomprehensible and deeply disturbing. What venom infected the killers' minds to compel them to take the life of another human? What injustice may have they suffered to warrant or even suggest such action? Were they so cavalier in their killing as to not even clearly identify their unfortunate victim? Are they so devoid of humanity that taking of another's life is meaningless to them?

Did the boy awake, aroused
Moments before his death
To see the dark intruders
Who shot him in his bed?

Remembering Nizzear (cont)

Did he recognize
With drowsy eyes and mind
The dim acquaintance
Who shot him in the head?

Did he raise a helpless hand
Or flash a troubled smile
Before his final breath
His last moment on this earth?

What grim satisfaction
Did the shooter take to see
Him sprawled and silent
His joyful life consumed in sudden death?

Will we think of him evermore
The bright young man, Nizzear
We never met and did not know
Each time we lock our door?

Rules of the Game

The rules are learnt in various ways
The game of life that each one plays
From parents' lips to skeptic ear
From book and bible and friendship dear
We live and learn with every breath
But who can teach the rules of death

The Late

Late to breakfast
Late for the school bus
Late all the rest of the day

So quickly all the days have flown
Still struggling to catch up
Soon to be late again

Emotaku

grief
stains
my pillow

fear
shouts
with anger's voice

touching
my heart
her fine fingers

On the Subject of Death

We joked and we laughed
until the very day he died.
How could I have known?

new openings
in the cold December earth
underground passage

while sleep descends
I wonder in the dark—how—
when will we part

Obituary

Did you know our friend
had nine children and a twin
played Hamlet on stage
and wrote columns for the Times?
I always meant to call him.

SIX

Something to Chew On

Sunday morning
sweet Port wine and eggs
remembering Dad

I like
my eggs on toast
she doesn't

tomato on toast
with mayo and lettuce
juice running down

savoring
a slice of sausage
forbidden fat

Dishes

when the guests have gone
stacking dishes quietly
until tomorrow
reticent to break the spell
of friendship's warm glow

washing and drying
yesterday's dirty dishes
while the soup simmers

Expectations

1. warm fingertips
   softly brushing my bare chest
   abrading my sleep
   her modest invitation
   our first morning after

2. no snow yet
   she hands me the Christmas wreath
   and smiles

3. at the red light
   I roll down the window
   hand him four singles
   he thanks me profusely
   but who should be thankful

Easter Morning

arriving early
to secure a front row pew
on Easter morning

mosaic windows
figures and symbols in glass
stained holy fragments

few empty places
as the faithful, finely dressed,
rarely seen, arrive

a visiting priest
invariant ritual
Will he have new jokes?

Easter Morning (cont)

happy gurgling
baby talk alleviates
a dreary homily

come to the water
a peaceful Easter hymn
for hopeful sinners

envelopes and cash
fill the collection basket
savings of sinners

leaving morning mass—
an hour of contemplation
and people watching

Easter Afternoon

yellow eggs and blue
pagan symbols celebrate
the resurrection

Choir Practice

The old preacher was darn near collapse
When he wandered one day, just perhaps,
Down the aisle toward the spire
And found all the choir
Playing craps on the floor of the apse

Moonstruck

the moon at midnight
your smiling face reflecting
your dark side hidden

the moon before dawn
floating luminescent globe
sinking through rooftops

A Stroll on the Beach

In late spring we travel from our home on the Georgia Piedmont to the Atlantic shore. For seven days our lives are suspended like sea gulls on the ocean breezes. We are reabsorbed into the vastness of nature, yet our small lives acquire more meaning rather than less.

Each morning we watch the hazy sun emerging from the rippled sea. Each morning the warm beach summons us to walk on its broad, compact sands beside the surging waters.

cloud streaked horizon
russet orb rising from the sea
morning coffee

shore birds skittering
pushing back the tide
breakfast on the beach

silent white condos
black eyes staring vacantly
at the roiling sea

shells on the beach
fragments shattered and worn
yesterday's dreams

strewn seaweed
remnants of the restless tide
furrows crease her brow

Hand-in-hand we leave the beach behind, silently wash down our sugared feet and return to reality.

Nocturnes

after the prom
our long, last embrace
reluctant sunrise

light more candelsh
she winks and grins
and pours more wine

a little scotch
at midnight
ice slowly melting

~~celebrating~~ observing
the dawn of a new year
stone sober

a fleeting shadow
hurries on
Did you see it too?

SEVEN

A vector is a quantity possessing magnitude and direction.

A scalar is a quantity such as mass or time, describable by a real number but without course or direction.

thankfully unknown
the scalar
to my life's vector

Space and Time

light from dead stars
through time and through space
falls on my face

peering into the vast darkness
I am
absorbed

Summer Harvest

If there is a heaven, may it be a small farm on the edge of the forest where golden eagles soar in the pale blue summer sky and fat, happy mice live in the granary, where fated flies dance hopelessly on long sticky strips tacked over the kitchen table. The table is laden at dinner time with fresh cow milk, hot yeast biscuits swimming with butter and other items of lesser importance, and the flickering light of a kerosene lantern repels shadows during the short, quiet wait between sunset and bed time.

I experienced this simple idyll in Northern Wisconsin when I was a young boy living the summer away from my home in the city. Remembrance of it never fails to revive the simultaneous antithetical emotions of tranquility and excitement. Except for a few enjoyable chores, the long, hot days were mine to spend in undirected discovery of small and large wonders of nature, butterflies and summer storms, to pump a cool, refreshing drink from the deep well, or pump The Death of Floyd Collins through the parlor player piano time after time after time, fly paper airplanes outside in the all-day rain, or climb into the hay mow to gaze at the barn rafters and let my imagination fly with the tiny sparrows.

Summer Harvest (cont)

The summer harvest is finally secured, the barns, cribs and silos filled to capacity, and the summertime orphan returns to his family in the distant city.

after the harvest
cool water in a tin cup
shadows of autumn

Introspection

Whose eyes are these that see me now?
The trusting toddler who saw all things anew,
The callow lad running, grinning, unaware
of tomorrow and tomorrow,
The striving science student with startling
universal insights, so it seemed then,
The shy young suitor with fragile heart,
The tall dark groom beholding his fair bride,
The proud new father
humbled by the infant in his arms,
The sorrowful son, at his mother's gravestone,
The troubled husband—
has love slipped away?

The poet, philosopher and family chronicler,
The aged crony with fleeting friends,
The gray-haired grandpa
grateful for their love,
The disappearing act:
Now you see me.
Now you don't.

Whose eyes are these
with clouded cataracts?

Holding On

sinking
into hopelessness
together

as you drift from me
I hold you closer
perhaps tomorrow

Twenty-Eight Days

What started insidiously as a vague malaise during lunch at a café and bar near the edge of town had not abated by the time we returned to our condo in the heart of Gatlinburg, Tennessee. Rather, by evening, the symptoms enlarged to become pronounced nausea and intermittent chills.

Dolly went to bed. I moved from sitting to lying positions on the couch, seeking some relief and comfort from the pain that had become increasingly intense. By 2 AM, doubled over with acute pain, I called 911.

The 15 mile, 30 minute ambulance trip to LeConte Medical Center in Sevierville felt like an eternity of torture. By 3:20 AM it was confirmed that my eighty-year-old appendix had burst—never a good sign. I managed to text our children a hurried heads-up by the time a general surgeon arrived,

At 4;00 AM, the bright blue lights of the OR greeted me, but I quickly went to black.

<u>Day 1</u>
I awaken in the dim light of the ICU, unaware of time, IV's bleeding drugs and fluids into my threatened body. Morphine and Zofran control the pain and nausea. Consciousness comes and goes. During one period of awareness, I meet the man who saved my life.

the surgeon declares
you are a lucky man
cheerful S. O. B.

Twenty-Eight Days (cont)

Day 4
I leave intensive care. The new room is bright and baren. The wounds of arthroscopic surgery are minimal and healing. I manage a step, then two. Later, I walk. OKAY. I am alive.
I want to go home.

Day 5
We need to run some tests and take X-rays.

white count up again
the surgeon frowns perplexedly
I am numb with fear

Day 7
A problem, he says, the one who cut the appendix from my bowel.
He frowns. White count won't come down, he says. Infection, I hear him say. Abscess. Staple line leak. Very rare.

I will open you
macho flyboy surgeon says
or else you will die

Day 14
Return to consciousness

Twenty-Eight Days (cont)

beside my cold bed
the night nurse tends her duties
do you want morphine?

unable to resist
narcotic psychedelics
gargoyles grin and mock

in my barren room
the aspirator hisses
lulling me to sleep

dawning consciousness
the knowledge that I live, and
I must die again

Day 21
Smiling visitors. Children. Grandchildren. You should name your new friend, they say, the hole in your side that empties your bowels into a bag.
I call it Oz.

I weep for my wife
for myself that was
I curse my ostomy

Twenty-Eight Days (cont)

Day 28
Goodbye, she says, helping me from the wheelchair.
Good luck.

I say goodbye
to the man I will
never see again

my gaunt face
dimly reflected
cannot smile

On each anniversary of my major medical misadventure, the sterile halls, the soft-spoken, diligent and sympathetic nurses of the life-saving LaConte Medical Center and the unfailing support of my wife and children remain vivid in my memory. I smile now, and I am grateful.

81

eighty-one today
out of bed at five AM
put on a red shirt

Old Poet's Lament

I'd guess that very few of you
Are wondering what it is you'll do
When, like me, you too
Are eighty-two.
Write haiku

As I've been known to do
With words so few
That do not rhyme?
Too little time.
So little time.

Or spread your words across the page
With raw emotion, joy or rage
Or just sit back, relax,
After all you've escaped the axe
Another year. Another day.

Gazing deep into the mirror
A stranger's face does now appear
With straggly hair and quite severe—
Oh dear, so queer,
So very queer.

Old Poet's Lament (cont)

Not my best year in retrospect
But, hey, I'm vertical, somewhat erect.
And bottom line: I'm feeling fine—
To think, to love, to do
To write a shaky line or two

On Facebook now and then,
At least in those brief moments when
My gray cells manage to engage,
Write something clever, even sage.
But on this day, my muse is shy

Perhaps she'll come back, by and by
And now, no matter how I try
To plan for an uncertain future
Conjure, muddle and conjecture
I just don't know what I will do

Now that I am really . . . eighty-two.

Eighty-Three

Another year, and now I'm eighty-three.

They say that exercise and diet are the key
to health, happiness and longevity.
Some even add a strong cup of green tea
and brew the wicked stuff religiously.

But I've come to know a tall glass of Chablis
is really much more satisfactory,
(especially with camembert or brie)
and filled donuts substitute for broccoli.

I haven't run a mile recently
and wouldn't ever think to climb a tree.
If I lift ten pounds accidentally
my muscles ache and cry out tragically.

It's not all bright with eyes that dimly see,
arthritis in both shoulders and one knee.
I might dose off while I stand to pee,
and hot romance—it's just a memory.

Eighty-Three (cont)

Though life may seem a challenge and a chore,
test your mind and your metal to the core,
grabbing your attention like a hungry lion's roar,
at least it's never, ever been a bore.

And when you're this old, perhaps you would agree
there's nowhere else that you would rather be.
If you please I'd like at least one more encore
to take a sagging senior shot at eighty-four.

Eleven fifty-nine

I pulled the quilt over her frail shoulders
(she is always cold)
and bent to smooch her cheek
(as I always do).
She said,
(offhand, as if she were mentioning
that she might be getting the sniffles)
I think I am ready to die now.

I enfolded her in my trembling arms
and stroked her sallow brow
I kissed her sunken cheek,
her soft sweet lips
and whispered hoarsely, no, no, no
you'll see tomorrow
will be better.

Eleven fifty-nine (cont)

How can I banish
that pernicious scene
from my thoughts?
That baleful memory
That crushing, bruising moment
that brings tears rushing hot into my eyes
even now, as I sit here in the dark
alone

Or when the cashier calls out
as I gaze into oblivion
Mister.
Mister.
Hey Mister
that will be
eleven fifty-nine.

Train Wreck

From laughter to tears
In the blink of an eye
And I don't know when
And I don't know why
I hurl out a curse
Or I whisper a prayer
Or whistle a tune
As if I didn't care
As if I really can bear
The burden of sorrow
That lies just beneath
Or rushes unbidden
From somewhere down deep
And I struggle to hide
What is really inside
So I tell her, I'm fine
It's all okay, until at last
At the end of the day
A brief respite when I sleep
If I sleep, perchance
To dream a dark dream
Or a sweet remembrance
Of a time gone by
Of a long lost time
When we didn't cry

Watch Out

If you sit in my chair
Please beware
It is my favorite
I really do savor it
And you will bask
In my glare

EIGHT

Ravens

A group of ravens is called an unkindness,
a conspiracy or a constable.

black birds jeering
taunting passersby
an unkindness

black birds huddle
quietly nodding
a conspiracy

black birds circling
enforcing their providence
a constable

Crows

A group of crows is called a murder or a congress.

*solemn black-robed crows
on the bank of the fish pond
contemplate murder*

*nodding their wisdom
the congress of crows
legislates nothing*

Journey's End

The sachem sits cross-legged at the entrance of the tribal lodge, gazing toward the edge of the great forest. The long rays of the rising sun warm his angular face. He is listening for the sound of wings.

The sound commences with a tentative flapping, testing the cool morning air. One bright bird rises from the trees, then ten more rise, circle and climb. The sound of beating wings increases as a hundred more birds ascend.

The village Indians, now awakened, stand at wigwam doors looking skyward in wonder at the annual miracle of nature. The sky is filled with birds. The sound of their flapping wings becomes a gentle, rolling thunder. The rays of the feeble morning sun, glinting red and gold on their rising bodies, is nearly blocked out by a thousand more birds, gathering in great gray clouds for their communal flight.

It is the third day of the great migration of the wild pigeon. For hours the autumn sky is filled with birds in flight as far as the eye can see. Before the sun sets, millions of the colorful birds, called passenger pigeons by the white man, will have flown over the village, over the great forests.

Journey's End (cont)

The year is 1810. Within one hundred years not one wild member of the most populous bird species on the American continent will remain. By 1910, the entire wild pigeon population of hundreds of millions of birds will fall prey to hunters and trappers and the destruction of their forest habitats.

The last of the species, Ectopistes migratoris, a female named Martha by her keepers, dies in the Cincinnati Zoo on the first day of September 1914.

Extinction.

restless wings now rest
the long journey ended
last of the species

finches bobbled flight
dandelions and pine cones
littering brown lawns

bird songs at dawn
fat raindrops spattering
slow awakening

Carolina Wren
chirping hopefully
tulips poking through

six fat strutting crows
on the neighbor's roof
stand in judgment

two cardinals
enclosed by the night
black as ravens

Gourmet Dog

There was an old dog from Hyde Park
Whose bite was worse than his bark
He thought those out of state
Didn't really taste great
But beware if you hail from New York

Dinosaur Divorce

There was a young brontosaurus named Doris
Who married a T-Rex named Boris
But their love making failed
And their marriage derailed
When he never could reach her clitoris

Moonlight Serenade

An old bullfrog from the lagoon
Sat on a rock and sang at the moon
A gator swallowed him down
Which made the frog frown
As he croaked, just a bit out of tune

After The Storm
(A dog's Tale)

Rub my belly. Scratch my ears.
Hold me close to quell my fears.
My voice is strong, but my spirit's frail
When I bark and wag my tail.
Cause I'm your puppy and you're my master
Protecting me from all disaster.

If the storm may come while you're not near
It makes me howl and shake with fear.
But if I poop upon the floor
You shout at me and hold the door.
I hope that you'll let me off the hook
When I sneak back in with a hang-dog look.

I did not mean to spoil your day.
If I knew how, I'd kneel and pray
That you'll forgive my little mistake
And realize how my heart does ache
While I wait and hope that you will still
Rub my belly and scratch my ears.

Fish Tale

There was a blue catfish named William
who lived in a giant aquarium
with Snark the shark,
four turtles and 65 other
Ichthyofauni.

Willy was puny and scrawny,
lived amongst weeds at the bottom.
Snark paid him no heed
while he swam through the weeds,
even the turtles ignored him.

Little Willy loved the aquarium floor
lacked any desire to travel
or explore what was above him
kept his nose in the gravel
with never a whim to swim to the brim.

Willy noticed some bubbles rising—
nothing really too surprising, but
unbeknownst to William,
as he rushed to gobble some up,
the bubbles consisted of Helium.

Fish Tale (cont)

Willy bit into one tiny bubble, then
gulped two big ones down whole.
Well, wouldn't you know, he started to rise
and float out of the weeds to the top,
bloated to five times his usual size.

When old Snark swam by
he gave fat Willy the eye
and decided to have a light lunch.
Down Willy went whole,
not a slurp or a burp or a crunch.

Poor Willy squirmed all the way down,
wiggled and jiggled and thought with a frown
If you munch gas on a lark
stay away from old Snark!
(Too late, yes, but profound.)

Old Snark the shark learned something too,
a simple lesson but most certainly true:
If you don't want to have gas
you had better pass
on fat catfish with a blue hue.

Frieda Croaks

The light of the moon
shone on the lagoon
so bright
it didn't seem night.
It might have been noon.

The fish and the frogs
started to play
just like it was day.
But not Ali
the grumpy old gator

who was rudely awoke
by Frieda Frog's croak.
Ali blinked his big eyes
and to Frieda's surprise
snapped open his jaws
and ate her.

Your Pick

When it comes to your face
You might want to erase
The assemblage
You got from your parents.

You don't get your druthers
Your chin is your mother's
And, happy or sad, eyes
And ears are your dad's.

You can't make the selection
Of which direction your tongue
Sticks out of your mouth
But you do get to pick
Your own nose.

Boris, the Talking Horse

My talking horse
(his name is Boris)
once caught equine diphtheria.

He sneezed a steed sneeze
started to wheeze and
became sad and morose
when his voice got so hoarse
I told him, Boris
I just cannot hear ya.

Medical Alert

Scope This Out

The proctologist nodded
as the long tube he prodded
into places that no one should see.
He winked with a grin
and shouted with glee
"We're just half way in
to your colonoscopy!"

Diagnosis

The radiologist said,
"It's all in your head
according to the arthroscope
So relax you big dope."

Aftershock

I still have the chills
though I took all my pills.
My head is chaotic
without antibiotic
But I'm sure I'll feel worse
when the doc sends his bills.

If

If boys
Were girls
Would they like to wear curls?

If girls
Were boys
Would they make lots of noise?

If the stupid
Were wise
Would the truth be all lies?

If a dog
Was a frog
Would it jump into a bog?

If a cat
Was a cur
Would it purr?

If a butterfly
Was a flybutter
Would it still flutter?

Stormy

When my dog, Stormy, hears thunder
he always dives under the bed.
I've told him that lightning
doesn't have to be frightening
but I can't get it into his head.

Suppose

Suppose
a rose
had a nose.
Would it
smell?

Stretching

early autumn frost
the sun stretches shadows
I stretch my legs

the pink jump suit
strains to contain its owner
waddling down the hall

Carter's
Pills
(bisacodyl)
(a stimulant laxative)

Carter' s
little liver pills
guaranteed to cure
your ills. Chill your fever.
Warm your chills.
Carter's little
liver pills

AFTERTHOUGHTS

well my dear old girl
can you still remember
the day we first met
the music we danced to
the wonder days
when we were young?

how lucky I have been
to have had you at my side
on our journey through life
to hold your hand now
to look back, to remember
and look for one more tomorrow.

today you said
I love you . . .
after all these years

ACKNOWLEDGEMENTS

Thanks to members of the Carrollton Creative Writers Club for their continuing support and encouragement and especially to those good friends in the Poetry Workshop for perceptive critiques and corrections as these works were in initial stages.
Special thanks to Chuck Wanager, Cecilia Lee, Robert Covel and Eleanor Hoomes for their careful reading of my manuscript and many helpful comments.

Thanks also to Amber D. Pickle for all her assistance with the book's cover, Seth Fitts of Whitesburg, Georgia for all the whimsical mice and John Bell of Vabella Publishing for all of his kind assistance.

Dailydoseofstuf.tumblr.com provided the cover photo.

The poems *Melody of Love* and *Summer Harvest* were previously published on the website
www.contemporaryhaibunonline.com.

PARTING SHOT

each new day
like a drop in the bucket
'til we kick it

REFERENCES

Just a few references if you want to know more about various poetic forms including haiku, haibun and tanka:

<u>About Poetry</u>
The Poetics of Japanese Verse, by Koji Kawamoto
Haiku in English (The first Hundred Years), edited by Jim Kacian, Phillip Rowland and Allan Burns
The Haiku Handbook, by William J. Higginson and Penny Harter
Ribbons, the triannual journal of the Tanka Society of American
The Disjunctive Dragonfly (a new approach to English language haiku), by Richard Gilbert
The Art and Craft of Poetry, by Michael J. Bugeja
Writing Personal Poetry, by Shelia Bender
<u>Select Few Favorite Books of Poems</u>
To Hear the Rain (haiku) by Peggy Lyles
The Plenitude of Emptiness (haibun) by Hortenia Anderson
Where the Sidewalk Ends by Shel Silverstein
The Trouble with Poetry by Billy Collins
We Almost Disappear by David Bottoms
Different Hours by Stephen Dunn
Leaves of Grass by Walt Whitman
Narrow Road to the Interior by Matsuo Basho
Contemporary Haibun Online,
www.contemporaryhaibunonline.com
Anything by Robert Frost, Edgar Allan Poe, Carl Sandburg, so many others . . . .

www.ingramcontent.com/pod-product-compliance
Lightning Source LLC
Chambersburg PA
CBHW061950070426
42450CB00007BA/1109